MEXICO 2016 HUMAN RIGHTS REPORT

Note: This report was updated 4/07/17; see Appendix F: Errata for more information.

EXECUTIVE SUMMARY

Mexico, which has 32 states, is a multiparty federal republic with an elected president and bicameral legislature. In 2012 President Enrique Pena Nieto of the Institutional Revolutionary Party (PRI) won election to a single six-year term in elections observers considered free and fair. Citizens elected members of the Senate in 2012 and members of the Chamber of Deputies in 2015. Observers considered the June gubernatorial elections free and fair.

Civilian authorities generally maintained effective control over the security forces.

The most significant human rights-related problems included involvement by police and military in serious abuses, such as unlawful killings, torture, and disappearances. Impunity and corruption in the law enforcement and justice system remained serious problems. Organized criminal groups killed, kidnapped, extorted, and intimidated citizens, migrants, journalists, and human rights defenders.

The following additional problems persisted: poor prison conditions; arbitrary arrests and detentions; intimidation and violence against human rights defenders and journalists; violence against migrants; violence against women; domestic violence; abuse of persons with disabilities; threats and violence against some members of the indigenous population; threats against lesbian, gay, bisexual, transgender, and intersex (LGBTI) persons; trafficking in persons; and child labor, including forced labor by children.

Impunity for human rights abuses remained a problem throughout the country with extremely low rates of prosecution for all forms of crimes.

Section 1. Respect for the Integrity of the Person, Including Freedom from:

a. Arbitrary Deprivation of Life and other Unlawful or Politically Motivated Killings

There were many reports the government or its agents committed arbitrary or unlawful killings, often with impunity. Organized criminal groups also were implicated in numerous killings, often acting with impunity and at times in league with corrupt state, local, and security officials. The National Human Rights Commission (CNDH) reported 27 complaints for "deprivation of life" between January and November.

On August 2, authorities arrested Juan Carlos Arreygue, the mayor of the municipality of Alvaro Obregon, and four police officers, including a commander, in connection with the killing of 10 persons detained by police on July 29. According to news reports, Alvaro Obregon police under instructions from the mayor, detained the civilians and executed them, later burning their bodies. The criminal investigation into the case continued at year's end.

In April a federal court charged the commander of the 97th Infantry Battalion and three other military officers for the July 2015 illegal detention and extrajudicial killing of seven suspected members of an organized criminal group in Calera, Zacatecas. No trial date had been set at year's end.

On August 18, the CNDH released a report that accused federal police of executing 22 persons after a gunfight in May 2015 near Tanhuato, Michoacan, and of tampering with evidence. The CNDH report concluded that two of the men killed were tortured and 13 were killed after they had been detained. One police officer was killed in the incident. National Security Commissioner Renato Sales Heredia claimed the officers acted in self-defense. In response to the CNDH report, President Enrique Pena Nieto removed Federal Police Chief Enrique Galindo from his position to allow for "an agile and transparent investigation." No federal police agents were charged, and the federal investigation continued at year's end.

Authorities made no additional arrests in connection with the January 2015 killing of 10 individuals and illegal detentions and injury to a number of citizens in Apatzingan, Michoacan.

In May a civilian federal judge acquitted and dismissed all charges against the remaining members of the military with pending charges in relation to the 2014 killings of 22 suspected criminals in Tlatlaya, State of Mexico. The court ruled that the evidence was insufficient to convict. In April the press reported that in October 2015 the Sixth Military Court dropped the charges against six soldiers and convicted one soldier, sentencing him to time served. In a report released in October 2015 before the verdicts, the CNDH determined that authorities arbitrarily deprived at least 12 to 15 of the civilians of life and tortured some of the witnesses. In July authorities of the State of Mexico declared they intended to fire nine state-level investigators from the General Prosecutor's Office and suspend 21 others for misconduct related to the case. Nongovernmental organizations (NGOs) expressed concerns regarding the lack of convictions in the case and the perceived failure to investigate the chain of command.

Former military corporal, Juan Ortiz Bermudez, appealed his 2015 conviction to 18 years' imprisonment for intentional homicide in the 2010 killing of two unarmed civilians in Nuevo Leon. Authorities had not scheduled a hearing at year's end.

Criminal organizations carried out human rights abuses and widespread killings throughout the country. For example, from July 9 to 15, criminal gangs executed several families in the northeastern state of Tamaulipas in what media reported as a war among drug-trafficking organizations. Criminals also targeted mayors (at least six killed this year) and other public officials. From 2006 to the middle of the year, 82 mayors were killed in the country.

News reports and NGO sources noted that from January 2015 to August, authorities discovered more than 724 bodies in several hundred clandestine graves throughout the country, the majority of killings were suspected to have been carried out by criminal organizations.

b. Disappearance

Federal law prohibits forced disappearances, but laws relating to forced disappearances vary widely across the 32 states and not all classify "forced disappearance" as distinct from murder or kidnapping. Investigation, prosecution, and sentencing for the crime of disappearance remained rare. The CNDH reported to the Inter-American Commission on Human Rights (IACHR) that as of October 2015, authorities opened 95 investigations at the state level for forced disappearances in nine states, resulting in four indictments but no convictions.

There were many reports of forced disappearances by security forces. There were numerous cases of disappearances related to organized criminal groups. In its data collection, the government often merged disappeared persons with missing persons, making it difficult to compile accurate statistics on the extent of the problem.

The CNDH registered 16 cases of alleged forced disappearances through the end of October.

The Office of the Attorney General of the Republic (PGR) revamped its Special Unit for Disappeared Persons in 2015, establishing expanded authorities and transferring 846 open cases from the predecessor PGR unit. The unit employed approximately 30 prosecutors and, as of May, was investigating the cases of 1,050 missing or disappeared persons. In June the attorney general appointed a prosecutor to lead the unit.

Authorities arrested 13 persons, including eight state police officers; they faced charges for the January 11 disappearance of five youths from Tierra Blanca, Veracruz. On February 8, federal authorities located the remains of two of the youths on a property reportedly used by drug traffickers after one officer admitted to the abduction and transfer of the youths to a local criminal gang. Several containers found there contained human remains estimated to belong to hundreds of victims killed over a period of several years.

On April 28, a 17-year-old boy disappeared in the state of Veracruz, with the alleged participation of the Veracruz state police called "Fuerza Civil." International NGOs reported that the boy's mother had difficulty filing the disappearance report with the state attorney general's office.

On November 10, the IACHR launched the follow-up mechanism agreed to by the government, the IACHR, and the families of the 43 students who disappeared in Iguala, Guerrero, in 2014. The government provided funding for the mechanism that follows up the work of the group of independent experts who supported the investigation of the disappearances and assisted the families of the victims from March 2015 to April 30. At the end of their mandate in April, the experts released a final report strongly critical of the government's handling of the case.

According to information provided by the PGR in November, authorities had indicted 168 individuals and arrested 128, including 73 police officers from Cocula and Iguala and 55 alleged members of the Guerrero-based drug trafficking organization, Guerreros Unidos. Representatives of civil society organizations and the IACHR-affiliated experts noted that authorities held many of those arrested on charges such as participation in a criminal organization but not on involvement in the students' disappearances. A CNDH report implicated federal police and local police officers from nearby Huitzuco. In October authorities arrested the former police chief of Iguala, who had been in hiding since the 2014 disappearances.

Both federal and state authorities continued at year's end to investigate the case, including the whereabouts of the missing students or their remains.

Kidnappings remained a serious problem for persons at all socioeconomic levels, and there were credible reports of instances of police involvement in kidnappings for ransom, often at the state and local level. The government's statistics agency (INEGI) estimated that 94 percent of crimes were either unreported or not investigated and that underreporting for kidnapping may be even higher.

Coahuila state authorities issued arrest warrants in June for 15 individuals--10 of whom were former police--for forced disappearances in the border state of Coahuila. According to state authorities, from 2009 to 2012, the Zetas transnational criminal organization, allegedly in collusion with local police, carried out mass disappearances in the border towns of Piedras Negras, Allende, and Nava. Elements of the organization allegedly killed some of the victims and disposed of their remains in Piedras Negras' state prison.

c. Torture and Other Cruel, Inhuman, or Degrading Treatment or Punishment

The law prohibits such practices and stipulates confessions obtained through illicit means are not admissible as evidence in court, but there were reports that government officials employed them.

There is no national registry of torture cases, and a lack of data on torture cases at the state level.

As of October 31, the CNDH registered 206 complaints of alleged torture and 451 cases of cruel, inhuman, or degrading treatment. NGOs stated that in some cases the CNDH misclassified torture as inhuman or degrading treatment.

News reports indicated that the PGR was examining 4,000 cases of torture in the first nine months of the year. The reports indicated that judges issued 14 arrest warrants for torture, including five arrest warrants for army and federal police members.

In June a report by Amnesty International accused security officials of using sexual and other types of torture to secure confessions from women.

On April 14, a video was posted on social media showing a woman being tortured by two soldiers and members of the Federal Police in an incident that took place in February 2015 in Ajuchitlan del Progreso, state of Guerrero. The secretary of defense, General Salvador Cienfuegos, made an unprecedented public apology. National Security Commissioner Renato Sales also offered a public apology. In January authorities detained two of the soldiers allegedly implicated, and they faced civilian charges of torture as well as military charges of disobeying orders. Authorities suspended members of the Federal Police for their involvement.

On January 20, a federal court in Ciudad Juarez, Chihuahua sentenced army Colonel Elfego Jose Lujan Ruiz (the former commander of the 35th Infantry Battalion in Nuevo Casas Grandes) to 33 years in prison for the 2009 torture, homicide, and clandestine burial of two men. Authorities also sentenced five other convicted former soldiers of the 35th Infantry Battalion; three to 33 years in prison for the same crimes and two to 39 months in prison for torture.

In April authorities sentenced army General Manuel Moreno Avina to 52 years' imprisonment for the torture, homicide, and destruction of human remains of a man in Chihuahua in 2008. The federal judge also ordered the Ministry of Defense (SEDENA) to offer a public apology and accept responsibility for killing the man. Media reported that, as of October 31, authorities sentenced 21 soldiers who were under Moreno's command on charges related to torture, homicide, drug trafficking, and other crimes.

Prison and Detention Center Conditions

Conditions in prisons and detention centers were often harsh and life threatening due to corruption, overcrowding, prisoner abuse, alcohol and drug addiction, and lack of security and control.

Civil society groups reported abuses of migrants in some detention centers.

Physical Conditions: In a report published during the year, the IACHR noted that federal and state detention centers suffered from "uncontrolled self-government in aspects such as security and access to basic services, violence among inmates, lack of medical attention, a lack of real opportunities for social reintegration, a lack of differentiated attention for groups of special concern, abuse by prison staff, and lack of effective grievance mechanisms."

There were numerous cases of corruption in the penitentiary system, including allegations of high-level corruption related to the July 2015 escape of Sinaloa cartel leader Joaquin "El Chapo" Guzman. The IACHR reported that 200 of the 388 penitentiary centers in the country were overcrowded. News reports indicated that Hidalgo State had the most overcrowded prisons and identified the district jail in Tepeaca, Puebla, as the most overcrowded (329 inmates in a jail designed for 49); 239 of the prisoners were awaiting their sentences. In April the CNDH reported that overcrowding in prisons was the main factor in lack of social rehabilitation. Health and sanitary conditions were poor, and most prisons did not offer psychiatric care. Some prisons often were staffed with poorly trained, underpaid, and corrupt correctional officers, and authorities occasionally placed prisoners in solitary confinement indefinitely. Prisoners often had to bribe guards to acquire food, medicine, and other necessities. In some cases prisoners reportedly had to pay a fee to be permitted to visit with family members. Authorities held pretrial detainees together with convicted criminals. The CNDH noted a lack of access to adequate health care was a significant problem. Food quality and quantity, heating, ventilation, and lighting varied by facility, with internationally accredited prisons generally having the highest standards.

The CNDH reported conditions for female prisoners, particularly for women who lived with their children in prison, were inferior to those for men, due to a lack of appropriate living facilities and specialized medical care. There were reports women who lived with their children in prison did not receive extra food or assistance.

The CNDH reported 52 homicides and 23 suicides in state and district prisons in 2015. The CNDH noted in its 2015 report on prisons that 86 prisons did not have a suicide prevention system. On February 11, 49 inmates were killed in the deadliest prison riot in history at the Nuevo Leon state prison of Topo Chico. In June, three prisoners were killed and 14 injured in another riot at the same prison. A senior Nuevo Leon state official cited poor prison conditions and a lack of funding as primary contributing factors for continued violence at the prison.

Administration: At some state prisons, recordkeeping remained inadequate. While prisoners and detainees could file complaints regarding human rights violations, access to justice was inconsistent, and authorities generally did not publicly release the results of investigations.

Independent Monitoring: The government permitted independent monitoring of prison conditions by the International Committee of the Red Cross, the CNDH, and state human rights commissions. Independent monitors were generally limited to making recommendations to authorities to improve prison conditions.

Improvements: In June a new law allowed women to have full custody of their children while in prison until the children reached three years of age.

On June 16, the National Criminal Enforcement Act went into effect, which defines the guiding principles of the prison system to be dignity, equality, legality, due process, transparency, confidentiality, and social reinsertion. The law points out that women require different accommodations than men and identifies the important role community contact plays in successful social reintegration.

Both federal and state facilities sought international accreditation from the American Correctional Association, which requires demonstrated compliance with a variety of international standards. As of September 1, 12 additional correctional facilities achieved association accreditation, bringing the total number of accredited facilities to 42.

d. Arbitrary Arrest or Detention

The law prohibits arbitrary arrest and detention, but the government often failed to observe these prohibitions.

Role of the Police and Security Apparatus

The federal police, as well as state and municipal police, have primary responsibility for law enforcement and the maintenance of order. The federal police are under the authority of the interior minister and the National Security Committee, state police are under the authority of each of the 32 governors, and municipal police are under the authority of local mayors. SEDENA, which oversees the army and air force, and the Ministry of the Navy (SEMAR), which oversees the navy and marines, also play a role in domestic security, particularly in combatting organized criminal groups. The National Migration Institute (INM), under the authority of the Interior Ministry (SEGOB), is the administrative body responsible for enforcing migration laws and protecting migrants. The INM's 5,400 agents worked at ports of entry, checkpoints, and detention centers, conducting migrant apprehension operations in coordination with the federal police.

The law requires military institutions to transfer all cases involving civilian victims, including human rights cases, to the civilian justice system under the jurisdiction of the PGR. If the victim is a member of the military, alleged perpetrators remain subject to the military justice system. SEDENA, SEMAR, the federal police, and the PGR have security protocols for the transfer of detainees, chain of custody, and use of force. The protocols, designed to reduce the time arrestees remain in military custody, outline specific procedures for handling detainees.

According to the Office of the Attorney General of Military Justice, as of April 18, the military had transferred to the civilian Attorney General's Office prosecutorial jurisdiction for more than 1,273 military personnel accused of human rights violations in 558 criminal cases, 257 homicide cases, 229 torture cases, and 72 forced disappearance cases. As of June SEDENA reported there were no cases before military courts that involved a civilian victim.

Although civilian authorities maintained effective control over security forces and police, impunity, especially for human rights abuses, remained a serious problem. The country had extremely low rates of prosecution, and prosecutions could take years to complete.

There were new developments in the 2006 San Salvador Atenco confrontation between local vendors and state and federal police agents in Mexico State during which two individuals were killed and more than 47 women were taken into custody with many allegedly sexually tortured by police officials. In 2009 an appeals court acquitted the only individual previously convicted in the case, and in September the Inter-American Court of Human Rights agreed to hear the case, but no date has been set.

By law elected officials enjoy immunity from prosecution, including for corruption, while they hold a public office, although state and federal legislatures have the authority to waive an elected official's immunity.

SEDENA's General Directorate for Human Rights investigates military personnel for violations of human rights identified by the CNDH and is responsible for promoting a culture of respect for human rights within the institution. The directorate, however, has no power to prosecute allegations or to take independent judicial action.

In May the code of military justice was reformed to establish procedures for the conduct of military oral trials, in accordance with the transition to an adversarial justice system. On June 15, the CNDH published and submitted to the Supreme Court a "Report of Unconstitutionality" in which it claimed aspects of the recently revised code of military justice and military code of criminal procedures (military code or CMPP) violated constitutional guarantees, including against unreasonable searches and seizures. The CNDH based its claims on provisions of the military code that allow military prosecutors to request permission from civilian prosecutors from the Attorney General's Office to intercept communications and search premises during the investigation of military personnel for ties to organized crime, murder, and weapons violations. The CNDH criticized the ability of a military judge to call a civilian to testify in military court, the requirement that authorities must conduct all procedural acts in Spanish, and the expanded roles given to the Military Ministerial Police (the top-level investigative entity of the military).

In February, SEMAR expanded its human rights program to include a weeklong course (from the previous one-day course), an intensive program for commanding officers, and a human rights diploma program, among others.

Arrest Procedures and Treatment of Detainees

The constitution allows any person to arrest another if the crime is committed in his or her presence. A warrant for arrest is not required if an official has direct evidence regarding a person's involvement in a crime, such as having witnessed the commission of a crime. Bail exists, except for persons held in connection with drug trafficking or other forms of organized crime. In most cases the law provides for detainees to appear before a judge, and for authorities to provide sufficient evidence to justify continued detention, within 48 hours of arrest, but there were violations of the 48-hour provision. In cases involving three or more parties to a conspiracy to commit certain crimes, authorities may hold suspects for up to 96 hours before being presented to a judge.

Only the federal judicial system may prosecute cases involving organized crime. Under a procedure known in Spanish as "arraigo" (a constitutionally permitted form of detention, employed during the investigative phase of a criminal case before probable cause is fully established), certain suspects may, with a judge's approval, be detained for up to 80 days prior to the filing of formal charges. Human rights NGOs claimed arraigo allowed some corrupt officials to extort detainees, detain someone, and then seek reasons to justify the detention, or obtain confessions using torture. In the absence of formal charges, persons detained under arraigo are often denied legal representation and are not eligible to receive credit for time served if convicted.

Some detainees complained about lack of access to family members and to counsel after police held persons incommunicado for several days and made arrests arbitrarily without a warrant. Police occasionally provided impoverished detainees counsel only during trials and not during arrests or investigations as provided for by law. Authorities held some detainees under house arrest.

Arbitrary Arrest: Allegations of arbitrary detentions persisted throughout the year. The IACHR, the UN Working Group on Arbitrary Detention, and NGOs expressed concerns regarding arbitrary detention and the potential for arbitrary detention leading to other human rights abuses.

Pretrial Detention: Lengthy pretrial detention was a problem. According to an IACHR report, SEGOB figures as of August 2015 noted that 107,441 of 254,469 individuals detained were in pretrial detention. According to an international NGO, more than 40 percent of prisoners were awaiting their trial at the end of 2015. The law provides time limits within which authorities must try an accused person. Authorities generally disregarded time limits on pretrial detention since caseloads far exceeded the capacity of the federal judicial system.

Detainee's Ability to Challenge Lawfulness of Detention before a Court: Persons who are arrested or detained, whether on criminal or other grounds, may challenge their detention through the Juicio de Amparo. The defense may argue, among other things, that the accused did not receive proper due process; suffered a human rights abuse; or that authorities infringed upon basic constitutional rights. By law individuals should obtain prompt release and compensation if found to be unlawfully detained, but the authorities did not always promptly release those unlawfully detained.

e. Denial of Fair Public Trial

Although the constitution and law provide for an independent judiciary, court decisions were susceptible to improper influence by both private and public entities, particularly at the state and local level. Authorities sometimes failed to respect court orders, and at the state and local levels, arrest warrants were sometimes ignored.

Trial Procedures

As of June the civilian and military courts officially transitioned from an inquisitorial legal system based primarily upon judicial review of written documents to an accusatory trial system reliant upon oral testimony presented in open court. While observers expected the new system would take several years to implement fully, the federal government and all of the states began to adopt it. In some states implementing the accusatory system, alternative justice centers employed mechanisms such as mediation, negotiation, and restorative justice to resolve minor offenses outside the court system.

Under the new system, all hearings and trials are conducted by a judge and follow the principles of public access and cross-examination. Defendants have the right to a presumption of innocence and to a fair and public trial without undue delay. Defendants have the right to attend the hearings and to challenge the evidence or testimony presented. Defendants have access to government-held evidence, although the law allows the government to keep elements of an investigation confidential until the presentation of evidence in court. Defendants may not be compelled to testify or confess guilt. The law also provides for the rights of appeal and of bail in many categories of crimes.

The law provides defendants with the right to an attorney of their choice at all stages of criminal proceedings. Attorneys are required to meet legal qualifications to represent a defendant. Not all public defenders had preparation and training to serve adequately on the defendants' behalf, and often the state public defender system was not adequate to meet demand. Public defender services functioned either in the judicial or executive branch. According to the Center for Economic Research and Economic Teaching (CIDE), most criminal suspects did not receive representation until after they came under judicial authority, thus making individuals vulnerable to coercion to sign false statements prior to appearing before a judge.

Although required by law, interpretation and translation services from Spanish to indigenous languages at all stages of the criminal process were not always available. Indigenous defendants who did not speak Spanish sometimes were unaware of the status of their cases and were convicted without fully understanding the documents they were allegedly required to sign.

Political Prisoners and Detainees

There were no reports of political prisoners or detainees. On August 13, authorities released antilogging activist Ildefonso Zamora from prison after a court dropped burglary charges against him. Human rights NGOs had criticized his 2015 arrest as politically motivated due to his antilogging activism.

Civil Judicial Procedures and Remedies

Citizens have access to an independent judiciary in civil matters to seek civil remedies for human rights violations. For a plaintiff to secure damages against a defendant, authorities first must find the defendant guilty in a criminal case, a significant barrier in view of the relatively low number of convictions for civil rights offenses.

f. Arbitrary or Unlawful Interference with Privacy, Family, Home, or Correspondence

The law prohibits such practices and requires search warrants. There were some complaints of illegal searches or illegal destruction of private property.

Section 2. Respect for Civil Liberties, Including:

a. Freedom of Speech and Press

The law provides for freedom of speech and press, and the government generally respected these rights. Most newspapers, television, and radio stations had private ownership. The government had minimal presence in the ownership of news media but remained the main source of advertising revenue. Media monopolies, especially on a local level, constrained freedom of expression.

Violence and Harassment: Journalists were sometimes subject to physical attacks, harassment, and intimidation due to their reporting. Perpetrators of violence against journalists continued to act with impunity with few reports of successful investigation, arrest, or prosecution of suspects. Observers believed organized crime to be behind some of these cases, but NGOs asserted there were significant instances when local government authorities participated in or condoned these acts. The international NGO Article 19 analyzed complaints of violence or harassment registered with their organization and reported that 47 percent of cases of aggression against journalists in the prior seven years originated from public officials.

According to the Office of the UN High Commissioner for Human Rights in Mexico, 14 journalists were killed between January and mid-December. During the first half of the year, Article 19 registered 218 cases of aggression against journalists, including assaults, intimidation, arbitrary detention, and threats; in 2015 there were 397 such cases.

On February 8, armed assailants kidnapped journalist Anabel Flores in her home in Veracruz. Authorities found her body the following day in neighboring Puebla State. NGOs asserted that moving her across state lines was meant to obstruct investigation of her death.

On June 20, unknown assailants shot and killed Elidio Ramos Zarate, a reporter for local Oaxaca newspaper *El Sur*, as he covered a demonstration allegedly led by teachers that included blockades. The victim and other reporters had received threats from masked individuals at the blockades. Article 19 had previously noted the vulnerability of reporters covering demonstrations, who were subject to attacks from both police and protesters. Two other journalists were killed in the state of Oaxaca.

On July 20, journalist Pedro Tamayo was killed outside his home in Veracruz--the third journalist killed in Veracruz between January and July. Tamayo had received threats previously; he had fled the state and was placed under police protection upon his return.

Censorship or Content Restrictions: Human rights groups reported state and local governments in some parts of the country worked to censor the media and threaten journalists. Journalists reported altering their coverage in response to a lack of protection from the government, attacks against members of the media and media facilities, false charges for publishing undesirable news, and threats or retributions against family, among other reasons. There were reports of journalists practicing self-censorship because of threats from criminal groups and of government officials seeking to influence or pressure the press, especially in the states of Tamaulipas and Sinaloa.

Libel/Slander Laws: Federal laws against defamation and slander were removed but remain on the books at the local level in some states. In April a Mexico City judge ruled against Sanjuana Martinez, a reporter who wrote an expose of politicians who allegedly patronized prostitutes. A politician named in the article sued Martinez for libel. Martinez was not notified of the lawsuit as required by law until a court ruled against her in April and ordered her to pay restitution.

<u>Nongovernmental Impact</u>: Organized criminal groups exercised a grave and increasing influence over media outlets and reporters, threatening individuals who published critical views of crime groups. Concerns persisted regarding the use of physical and digital violence by organized criminal groups in retaliation for information posted online, which exposed journalists, bloggers, and social media users to the same level of violence as that faced by traditional journalists.

<u>Actions to Expand Press Freedom</u>: Since its creation in late 2012 through September, the National Mechanism to Protect Human Rights Defenders and Journalists ("the mechanism") had accepted 367 cases--208 of them from journalists--out of 443 requests. NGOs noted that in the same period there were more than 1,800 attacks against journalists. SEGOB stated that since the establishment of the mechanism, there had not been a murder or forced disappearance of anyone protected under the mechanism. Separately, the Office of the Special Prosecutor for Crimes Against Freedom of Expression, part of the PGR, reported it continued training public servants and journalists on the importance of freedom of expression. During the year it did not prosecute any crimes committed against journalists.

Internet Freedom

The government did not restrict or disrupt access to the internet or block or filter online content. According to Freedom House, however, the government increased requests to social media companies to remove content. Freedom House's 2015 Freedom of the Net Report categorized the country's internet as partly free.

Some civil society organizations alleged that various state and federal agencies sought to monitor private online communications. NGOs alleged that provisions in secondary laws threatened the privacy of internet users by forcing telecommunication companies to retain data for two years, providing real-time geolocation data to police, and allowing security agents to obtain metadata from private communications companies without a court order. Furthermore, the law does not fully define the "appropriate authority" to carry out such actions.

An estimated 45 percent of citizens--approximately 58 million persons--used the internet as of July.

Academic Freedom and Cultural Events

There were no government restrictions on academic freedom or cultural events.

b. Freedom of Peaceful Assembly and Association

The law provides for the freedoms of assembly and association, and the government generally respected these rights. There were some reports of security forces using excessive force against demonstrators.

c. Freedom of Religion

See the Department of State's *International Religious Freedom Report* at www.state.gov/religiousfreedomreport/.

d. Freedom of Movement, Internally Displaced Persons, Protection of Refugees, and Stateless Persons

The law provides for freedom of internal movement, foreign travel, emigration, and repatriation, and the government generally respected these rights.

The government cooperated with the Office of the UN High Commissioner for Refugees (UNHCR) and other humanitarian organizations in providing protection and assistance to internally displaced persons, refugees, returning refugees, asylum seekers, stateless persons, or other persons of concern.

The government and press reports noted a marked increase in refugee and asylum applications over the previous year. A reported 2,100 migrants requested refugee status in the first four months of the year, compared with a total of 3,424 in 2015.

At the Iztapalapa detention center near Mexico City and other detention centers, including in Chiapas, men were kept separate from women and children, and there were special living quarters for LGBTI individuals. Migrants had access to medical, psychological, and dental services, and the Iztapalapa center had agreements with local hospitals for any urgent cases free of charge. Those from countries with consular representation also had access to consular services. The National Refugee Commission (COMAR) and CNDH representatives visited daily, and other established civil society groups were able to visit the detention facilities on specific days and hours. The INM and Children and Family Services' officials took trafficking and other victims to designated shelters. Human rights pamphlets were available in many different languages.

<u>Abuse of Migrants, Refugees, and Stateless Persons</u>: The press and NGOs reported victimization of migrants by criminal groups and, to a lesser extent, by police and immigration officers and customs officials. Government and civil society sources reported Central American gang presence spread farther into the country and threatened migrants who had fled the same gangs in their home countries. On March 3, the Supreme Court ordered the Attorney General's Office to allow the families access to the files of the 2010 killings of 72 migrants in San Fernando, Tamaulipas. Since August 2014 the INM had turned over to state and federal prosecution authorities approximately 1,110 individuals suspected of having committed a crime against migrants.

In March the government began operating the Crimes Investigation Unit for Migrants and the Mexican Foreign Support Mechanism of Search and Investigation. The International Organization for Migration collaborated with municipal governments to establish offices along the border with Guatemala to track and assist migrants.

<u>In-country Movement</u>: There were numerous instances of armed groups limiting the movements of migrants, including by kidnappings and homicides.

Internally Displaced Persons

The Internal Displacement Monitoring Center estimated that as of December 2015, there were at least 287,000 internally displaced persons (IDPs), which resulted primarily from several displacement events that forced persons to flee their homes and communities in response to criminal, political, and religious violence as well as natural disasters. In May the CNDH released a report stating that 35,433 IDPs were displaced due to drug trafficking violence, religious conflicts, and land disputes. Tamaulipas reportedly had the highest number of IDPs at approximately 20,000, followed by Guerrero with 2,165, and Chihuahua with 2,008. NGO estimates of IDP numbers were higher: hundreds of thousands of citizens, many fleeing areas of armed conflict among organized criminal groups, or between the government and organized criminal groups, became internally displaced.

Protection of Refugees

<u>Access to Asylum</u>: The law provides for the granting of asylum or refugee status and complementary protection, and the government has an established procedure for determining refugee status and providing protection to refugees. During the year COMAR increased refugee status recognition by 60 percent. In the summer

the INM entered into an agreement with UNHCR to relinquish custody to UNHCR those migrants who, while in INM custody, claimed a need for asylum. As of August 31 the INM had turned over approximately 200 persons to UNHCR.

Section 3. Freedom to Participate in the Political Process

The law provides citizens the ability to choose their government through free and fair periodic elections based on universal and equal suffrage and conducted by secret ballot to assure the free expression of the will of the people.

Elections and Political Participation

Recent Elections: Observers considered the June gubernatorial races in 12 states and local races in 13 states and the 2011 and 2015 legislative and 2012 presidential elections to be free and fair.

Participation of Women and Minorities: A 2014 constitutional reform requires parties to select equal numbers of women and men to run for seats in the Senate, the Chamber of Deputies, and state congresses. The law also requires that each candidate's substitute be of the same gender as the candidate to prevent instances of women gaining office and then stepping down so a male substitute can take the position, previously a common practice. Women held approximately 36 percent of Senate seats and 32 percent of federal deputy seats.

No laws limit the participation of women and members of minorities in the process and women and minorities did so. There were no established quotas for increased participation of indigenous groups in the legislative body, and no reliable statistics were available regarding minority participation in government. The law provides for the right of indigenous people to elect representatives to local office according to "uses and customs" law rather than federal and state electoral law.

Section 4. Corruption and Lack of Transparency in Government

The law provides criminal penalties for conviction of official corruption, but the government did not enforce the law effectively. There were numerous reports of government corruption during the year. Corruption at the most basic level involved paying bribes for routine services or in lieu of fines to administrative officials and security forces. More sophisticated and less apparent forms of corruption included overpaying for goods and services to provide payment to elected officials and political parties.

By law all applicants for federal law enforcement jobs (and other sensitive positions) must pass a vetting process upon entry into service and every two years thereafter throughout their careers. According to SEGOB and the National Center of Certification and Accreditation, most active police officers at the national, state, and municipal level underwent at least initial vetting. The press and NGOs reported that police who failed vetting remained on duty. The CNDH reported that police, particularly at the state and local level, were involved in kidnapping, extortion, and providing protection for, or acting directly on behalf of, organized crime and drug traffickers.

During the year the government adopted a new National Anticorruption System that gives autonomy to federal administrative courts to investigate and sanction administrative acts of corruption, establishes harsher penalties for corrupt government officials, provides the Superior Audit Office (ASF) with real-time auditing authority, and establishes an oversight commission with civil society participation. Observers hailed the legislation as a major achievement in the fight against corruption, although some NGOs criticized the provision that allows public servants to opt out of declaring assets.

Corruption: In October the PGR indicted and issued an arrest warrant for the governor of Veracruz who went into hiding. In midyear the ASF filed criminal charges with the Attorney General's Office against 14 state governments for misappropriation of billions of dollars in federal funds. The ASF also investigated several state governors, including the former governors of Chihuahua, Quintana Roo, Sonora, and Nuevo Leon. The investigations continued at year's end.

Financial Disclosure: In July the Congress passed a law requiring all federal and state-level appointed or elected officials to provide income and asset disclosure, statements of any potential conflicts of interests, and tax returns, though it is possible to opt-out of making the information available to the public. The Ministry of Public Administration monitors disclosures with support from each agency. Regulations require disclosures at the beginning and end of employment, and also require yearly updates. The law requires declarations be made publicly available unless the official petitions for a waiver to keep them private. Criminal or administrative sanctions apply for abuses. Opposition political parties petitioned the Supreme Court in midyear to overturn the section of the law that would allow officials a waiver to keep the disclosures private.

<u>Public Access to Information</u>: A 2015 law grants free public access to government information at the state and federal levels. Authorities implemented the law effectively at the federal level and continued to work on harmonizing state-level laws for implementation in the states. The law includes exceptions to disclosure of government information, including for information that may compromise national security, affect the conduct of foreign relations, harm the country's financial stability, endanger another person's life, or for information relating to pending law enforcement investigations. The law also limits disclosure of personal information to third parties.

Section 5. Governmental Attitude Regarding International and Nongovernmental Investigation of Alleged Violations of Human Rights

A variety of domestic and international human rights groups generally operated without government restriction, investigating and publishing their findings on human rights cases. Government officials were mostly cooperative and responsive to their views, and the president or cabinet officials met with human rights organizations such as the Office of the UN High Commissioner for Human Rights, the IACHR, and the CNDH. Some NGOs alleged that individuals who organized campaigns to discredit human rights defenders sometimes acted with tacit support from officials in government.

<u>Government Human Rights Bodies</u>: The CNDH is a semiautonomous federal agency created by the government and funded by the legislature to monitor and act on human rights violations and abuses. It may call on government authorities to impose administrative sanctions or pursue criminal charges against officials, but it is not authorized to impose penalties or legal sanctions. Whenever the relevant authority accepts a CNDH recommendation, the CNDH is required to follow up with the authority to verify that it is carrying out the recommendation. The CNDH sends a request to the authority asking for evidence of its compliance and includes this follow-up information in its annual report. When authorities fail to accept a recommendation, the CNDH makes that failure known publicly and may exercise its power to call before the Senate government authorities who refuse to accept or enforce its recommendations.

All of the country's 32 states have their own human rights commission. The legislatures fund state-level commissions and instruct them to be autonomous. The state commissions did not have the same reporting requirements, making nationwide statistics difficult to compile and compare. The CNDH can take cases from state-level commissions if it receives a complaint the commission has not adequately investigated.

Section 6. Discrimination, Societal Abuses, and Trafficking in Persons

Women

<u>Rape and Domestic Violence</u>: Federal law criminalizes rape, including spousal rape, and conviction carries penalties of up to 20 years' imprisonment. Twenty-four states have laws criminalizing spousal rape. Human rights organizations asserted authorities at times did not take seriously reports of rape, and victims were socially stigmatized and ostracized.

The federal penal code prohibits domestic violence and stipulates penalties for conviction of between six months' and four years' imprisonment. Twenty-nine states stipulate similar penalties, although sentences in practice were often more lenient. Federal law does not criminalize spousal abuse. State and municipal laws addressing domestic violence largely failed to meet the required federal standards and often were unenforced, although states and municipalities, especially in the north, were beginning to prioritize training on domestic violence.

Victims of domestic violence in rural and indigenous communities often did not report abuses due to fear of spousal reprisal, stigma, and societal beliefs that abuse did not merit a complaint.

According to the law, femicide--the killing of a woman based on her gender--is a federal offense punishable by 40 to 60 years in prison. It is also an offense listed in the criminal codes of all states. The Special Prosecutor's Office for Violence against Women and Trafficking in Persons of the PGR is responsible for leading government programs to combat domestic violence and prosecuting federal human trafficking cases involving three or fewer suspects. The office had 40 federal prosecutors dedicated to federal cases of violence against women, approximately 15 of whom specialized in trafficking countrywide.

In 2015 and 2016, the federal government began using a "gender alert" mechanism that has existed at the federal level since 2007. The declaration of a gender alert directs relevant local, state, and federal authorities to take immediate action to combat violence against women by granting victims legal, health, and psychological services, and speeding investigations of unsolved cases. Since July 2015 the federal government has activated gender alerts in three states: Mexico,

Morelos, and Michoacan. The state government of Jalisco activated its own gender alert. Civil society groups complained that so far the alerts had not led to noticeable changes.

In collaboration with civil society, the state of Mexico established the country's first "gender alert" system to collect information to support investigations of gender-based violence in 11 of the 125 municipalities. At the national level, there were 72 shelters, of which civil society organizations operated 34, private welfare institutions operated four, and 34 were public institutions.

Sexual Harassment: Federal labor law prohibits sexual harassment and provides for fines from 250 to 5,000 times the minimum daily wage. Sixteen states criminalize sexual harassment, and all states have provisions for punishment when the perpetrator is in a position of power. According to the National Women's Institute (INMUJERES), the federal institution charged with directing national policy on equal opportunity for men and women, sexual harassment in the workplace was a significant problem, but victims were reluctant to come forward, and cases were difficult to prove.

Reproductive Rights: Couples and individuals have the right to decide the number, spacing, and timing of their children; manage their reproductive health; and have the information and means to do so, free from discrimination, coercion, or violence.

There were some reports of women pressured to undergo involuntary sterilization, including among indigenous populations, patients afflicted with HIV, and inmates. Antiretroviral therapy to prevent mother-to-child HIV transmission was available.

Discrimination: The law provides women the same legal status and rights as men and "equal pay for equal work performed in equal jobs, hours of work, and conditions of efficiency." According to INMUJERES women earned between 5 and 30 percent less than men for comparable work, whereas the World Economic Forum reported women earned 43 percent less than men for comparable work. Women were more likely to experience discrimination in wages, working hours, and benefits.

Children

Birth Registration: Children derived citizenship both by birth within the country's territory and from one's parents. Citizens generally registered the births of newborns with local authorities. In some instances government officials visited private health institutions to facilitate the process. Failure to register births could result in the denial of public services, such as education or health care.

Child Abuse: There were numerous reports of child abuse. In December 2015 the government created a National Program for the Integral Protection of Children and Adolescents, mandated by law, which is responsible for coordinating the protection of children's rights at all levels of government. The program includes the creation of a National System of Information on Children and Adolescents, designed to improve data on treatment of children.

Early and Forced Marriage: The legal minimum marriage age is 18. Enforcement, however, was inconsistent across the states, where some civil codes permit a minimum marital age of 14 for girls and 16 for boys with parental consent, and 18 without parental consent. With a judge's consent, children may marry at younger ages.

Sexual Exploitation of Children: The law prohibits the commercial sexual exploitation of children, and authorities generally enforced the law. Nonetheless, NGOs reported sexual exploitation of minors, as well as child-sex tourism in resort towns and northern border areas.

Statutory rape constitutes a crime in the federal criminal code. If an adult has sexual relations with a minor between ages 15 and 18, the penalty is between three months and four years in prison. Conviction of sexual relations with a minor under age 15 is liable to a penalty ranging from eight to 30 years' imprisonment. Laws against corruption of a minor and child pornography apply to victims under age 18. For conviction of the crimes of selling, distributing, or promoting pornography to a minor, the law stipulates a prison term of six months to five years and a fine of 300 to 500 times the daily minimum wage. For conviction of crimes involving minors in acts of sexual exhibitionism or the production, facilitation, reproduction, distribution, sale, and purchase of child pornography, the law mandates seven to 12 years' imprisonment and a fine of 800 to 2,500 times the daily minimum wage.

Perpetrators convicted of promoting, publicizing, or facilitating sexual tourism involving minors face seven to 12 years' imprisonment and a fine of 800 to 2,000 times the daily minimum wage. For those convicted of involvement in sexual tourism who commit sexual acts with minors, the law requires a 12- to 16-year prison sentence and a fine of 2,000 to 3,000 times the daily minimum wage. The crime of sexual exploitation of a minor carries an eight- to 15-year prison sentence and a fine of 1,000 to 2,500 times the daily minimum wage. The crimes of child sex tourism and exploiting of children in prostitution do not require a complaint to prosecute and can be based on anonymous information.

Institutionalized Children: Civil society groups expressed concerns regarding abuses of children with mental and physical disabilities in orphanages, migrant centers, and care facilities.

International Child Abductions: The country is party to the 1980 Hague Convention on the Civil Aspects of International Child Abduction. For information see the Department of State's *Annual Report on International Parental Child Abduction* at travel.state.gov/content/childabduction/en/legal/compliance.html.

Anti-Semitism

According to the 2010 census, the Jewish community numbered approximately 67,000 persons, 90 percent of whom lived in Mexico City. Jewish community leaders estimated there were closer to 45,000 Jews in the country. The Jewish community experienced low levels of anti-Semitism, which primarily involved anti-Semitic rhetoric in the media. In May the Jewish community reported that a congressman used anti-Semitic language during a live radio interview to denounce the candidacy of a Jewish leader as an advisor to the Human Rights Commission in Mexico City.

Trafficking in Persons

See the Department of State's *Trafficking in Persons Report* at www.state.gov/j/tip/rls/tiprpt/.

Persons with Disabilities

The law prohibits discrimination against persons with physical, sensory, intellectual, and mental disabilities in employment, education, air travel and other transportation, access to health care, the judicial system, and the provision of other services. The government did not effectively enforce the law. The law requires the Ministry of Health to promote the creation of long-term institutions for persons with disabilities in distress, and the Ministry of Social Development (SEDESOL) must establish specialized institutions to care for, protect, and house persons with disabilities in poverty, neglect, or marginalization. NGOs reported authorities had not implemented programs for community integration. NGOs reported no changes in the mental health system to create community services nor any efforts by authorities to have independent experts monitor human rights violations in psychiatric institutions.

Public buildings and facilities continued to be in noncompliance with the law requiring access for persons with disabilities. The education system provided special education for students with disabilities nationwide. Children with disabilities attended school at a lower rate than those without disabilities. NGOs reported employment discrimination.

Human rights abuses in mental health institutions and care facilities, including those for children, continued to be a problem. Abuses of persons with disabilities included lack of access to justice, the use of physical and chemical restraints, physical and sexual abuse, disappearances, and illegal adoption of institutionalized children. Institutionalized persons with disabilities often lacked adequate privacy and clothing and often ate, slept, and bathed in unhygienic conditions. They were vulnerable to abuse from staff members, other patients, or guests at facilities where there was inadequate supervision. Documentation supporting the person's identity and origin was lacking, and there were instances of disappearances.

As of October 31, the NGO Disability Rights International (DRI) reported that most residents had been moved to other institutions from the privately run institution Casa Esperanza, where they were allegedly victims of pervasive sexual abuse by staff and, in some cases, human trafficking. DRI reported that they were still suffering abuse and not receiving adequate treatment at these new institutions. Two of the victims died within the first six months after transfer to other facilities, one of whom was a victim of sexual abuse. DRI stated the victim was raped during a period of seven months in the new institution called Fundacion PARLAS I.A.P., and another woman was physically abused at the same institution. DRI claimed the government has not acted to improve conditions at these homes.

Persons with disabilities have the right to vote and participate in civic affairs. Voting centers for federal elections were generally accessible for persons with disabilities, and ballots were available with a braille overlay for federal elections. In Mexico City voting centers were also reportedly accessible for local elections, including braille overlays, but these services were inconsistently available for local elections elsewhere in the country.

Indigenous People

The constitution provides all indigenous people the right to self-determination, autonomy, and education. Although the law recognizes indigenous rights, indigenous groups reported the country's legal framework did not respect the property rights of indigenous communities or prevent violations of human rights. Most conflicts arose from interpretation of the "uses and customs" laws used by indigenous communities. Uses and customs laws apply traditional practices to resolve disputes, choose local officials, and collect taxes with limited federal or state government involvement. Communities and NGOs representing indigenous groups reported the government often failed to consult indigenous communities adequately when making decisions regarding the development of projects intended to exploit the energy, minerals, timber, and other natural resources on indigenous lands. The CNDH maintained a formal human rights program to inform and assist members of indigenous communities.

The CNDH reported indigenous women were among the most vulnerable groups in society. They experienced racism, discrimination, and violence. Indigenous persons generally had limited access to health and education services. The CNDH stressed past government actions to improve the living conditions of indigenous people, namely social programs geared specifically to women, were insufficient to overcome the historical marginalization of indigenous populations.

The law provides for educational instruction in the national language, Spanish, without prejudice to the protection and promotion of indigenous languages, but many indigenous children spoke only their native languages. The lack of textbooks and teaching materials, as well as the lack of qualified teachers fluent in these languages, limited education in indigenous languages.

In April indigenous communities in Chiapas along the border with Guatemala protested a hydroelectric project they claimed threatened to displace them.

In June the CNDH criticized immigration authorities for the 2015 detention of four citizens of indigenous descent for nine days by immigration officers in Queretaro who claimed they thought the four were Guatemalan.

Acts of Violence, Discrimination, and Other Abuses Based on Sexual Orientation and Gender Identity

The law prohibits discrimination against LGBTI individuals, but there were reports that the government did not always investigate and punish those complicit in abuses, especially outside Mexico City. Transgender persons may change their gender marker on identity documents only in Mexico City. The law prohibits discrimination based on sexual orientation, but only in Mexico City does it prohibit discrimination based on gender identity. Discrimination based on sexual orientation and gender identity was prevalent, despite a gradual increase in public tolerance of LGBTI individuals according to public opinion surveys. In March, Rubi Suarez Araujo became the first transgender municipal councilor, in Guanajuato.

In Mexico City the law criminalizes hate crimes based on sexual orientation and gender identity. Civil society groups claimed police routinely subjected LGBTI persons to mistreatment while in custody. Civil society groups reported that the full extent of hate crimes, including killings of LGBTI persons, was difficult to ascertain because authorities often mischaracterized these crimes as "crimes of passion," which resulted in the authorities' failure to adequately investigate, prosecute, or punish these incidents. The Executive Committee for Victims Assistance, an independent federal agency, completed a survey 425 lesbian, gay, bisexual or transgender persons. Seven of 10 respondents reported discrimination in schools; half reported employment discrimination or harassment; and six of 10 reported having known an LGBT person murdered in the past three years.

In October the press reported three killings of transgender individuals in the space of 13 days. NGOs stated transgender individuals faced discrimination and were marginalized even within the lesbian and gay community.

The National Council to Prevent Discrimination has both national and local level branches. The local council in Mexico City is the city government agency with the authority to resolve complaints of discrimination that occur within Mexico City. The national level council received complaints of discriminatory acts in areas of employment, access to commercial establishments, and access to education and health care. Civil society groups reported difficulty in determining whether individual complaints were ever resolved.

In January the Supreme Court ruled unanimously that denying same-sex partners the right to marry in the state of Jalisco was unconstitutional. A federal tribunal in Nuevo Leon ruled in favor of two women who fought for more than two years in court for the right to marry each other legally in the state. On February 14, the same-sex couple was the first to marry in Nuevo Leon through a civil ceremony in Monterrey. The court ruled in favor of the couple after the Supreme Court declared unconstitutional the state's civil code restricting marriage to a man and a woman.

Other Societal Violence or Discrimination

There were reports criminal groups kidnapped undocumented migrants to extort money from migrants' relatives or force them into committing criminal acts on their behalf.

The Catholic Multimedia Center reported criminal groups targeted priests and other religious leaders in some parts of the country and subjected them to extortion, death threats, and intimidation. There were multiple reports of priests kidnapped and killed. In early October the center stated there was an increase in the number of priests killed, from two in 2015 to seven during the year.

Self-defense groups--organized groups of armed civilians that claimed to fight crime in the face of inaction by governmental authorities--were concentrated in the southwestern states of Michoacan and Guerrero.

Section 7. Worker Rights

a. Freedom of Association and the Right to Collective Bargaining

The law provides for the right of workers to form and join unions, to bargain collectively, and to strike in both the public and private sectors; however, conflicting law, regulations, and practice restricted these rights.

The law requires a minimum of 20 workers to form a union. To receive official recognition from the government, unions must file for registration with the appropriate conciliation and arbitration board (CAB) or the Ministry of Labor and Social Welfare (STPS). For the union to be able to perform its legally determined functions, its leadership must also register with the appropriate CAB or STPS. CABs operated under a tripartite system with government, worker, and employer representatives. Outside observers raised concerns that the boards did not adequately provide for inclusive worker representation and often perpetuated a bias against independent unions, in part due to intrinsic conflicts of interest within the structure of the boards exacerbated by the prevalence of representatives from "protection" (unrepresentative, corporatist) unions.

By law a union may call for a strike or bargain collectively in accordance with its own bylaws. Before a strike may be considered legal, however, a union must file a "notice to strike" with the appropriate CAB, which may find that the strike is "nonexistent," or in other words, cannot proceed legally. The law prohibits employers from intervening in union affairs or interfering with union activities, including through implicit or explicit reprisals against workers. The law allows for reinstatement of workers if the CAB finds the employer fired the worker unfairly and the worker requests reinstatement; however, the law also provides for broad exemptions for employers from such reinstatement, including employees of confidence or workers who have been in the job for less than a year.

Although the law authorizes the coexistence of several unions in one worksite, it limits collective bargaining to the union that has "ownership" of a collective bargaining agreement. When there is only one union present, it automatically has the exclusive right to bargain with the employer. Once a collective bargaining agreement is in place at a company, another union seeking to bargain with the employer must compete for bargaining rights through a "recuento" (bargaining-rights election) administered by the CAB. The union with the largest number of votes goes on to "win" the collective bargaining rights. It is not mandatory for a union to consult with workers or have worker support to sign a collective bargaining agreement with an employer. The law establishes that internal union leadership votes may be held via secret ballot, either directly or indirectly.

The government, including the CABs, did not consistently protect worker rights. The government's common failure to enforce labor and other laws left workers with little recourse regarding violations of freedom of association, poor working conditions, and other labor problems. The CABs' frequent failure to impartially and transparently administer and oversee procedures related to union activity, such as union elections and strikes, undermined worker efforts to exercise freely their rights to freedom of association and collective bargaining. A report released in April 2015--commissioned by the President's Office and produced by the CIDE economic research center--found no guarantees of impartial and efficient labor justice from the boards and recommended the eventual incorporation of the CABs into the judicial branch.

In November the Congress passed constitutional reforms introduced in by President Pena Nieto that would dissolve the CABs and transfer their various functions to different entities. Judicial functions would transfer to the federal and state judiciaries, administrative functions would transfer to a new federal administrative entity, and conciliation functions would transfer to new conciliation entities. In addition to structural changes, the proposed labor reforms would require verification of worker support for a collective bargaining agreement prior to its registration, and they would establish concrete timeframes for all steps in the process for challenging a union's exclusive bargaining rights. Thirteen state legislatures approved the legislation prior to the end of the year.

By law penalties for violations of freedom of association and collective bargaining laws range from 16,160 pesos ($960) to 161,600 pesos ($9,640). Such penalties were rarely enforced and were insufficient to deter violations. Administrative and/or judicial procedures were subject to lengthy delays and appeals.

To reduce backlogs and average time to issue labor rulings from 200 to 150 days, some states began implementing oral trials at their local CABs. There are 19 CABs located in the states of Mexico, Hidalgo, and Baja California. In the state of Mexico, from 2011 to 2015, the new process reduced the number of pending actions from 35,000 to 27,000.

Workers exercised their rights to freedom of association and collective bargaining with difficulty. The process for registration of unions has been politicized, and according to union organizers, the government, including the CABs, frequently used the process to reward political allies or punish political opponents. For example, it rejects registration applications for new locals of independent unions and for new unions on technicalities.

Companies and protection unions used complex divisions and a lack of coordination between federal and state jurisdictions to manipulate the labor conciliation and arbitration processes. For example, a company might register a collective bargaining agreement at both the federal and the local level, and later alternate the jurisdictions when individuals filed and appealed complaints to gain favorable outcomes. Additionally, union organizers from several sectors raised concerns regarding the overt and usually hostile involvement of the CABs when organizers attempted to create independent unions.

Protection (unrepresentative, corporatist) unions and "protection contracts," collective bargaining agreements signed by employers and these unions to prevent meaningful negotiations and ensure labor peace, continued to be a problem in all sectors. These contracts were facilitated by exclusivity in bargaining and lack of a requirement for workers to demonstrate support for a collective bargaining agreement or the union that negotiated it before the agreement could take effect. Protection contracts often were developed before the company hired any workers and without direct input from or knowledge of the covered workers. For example, in August 2015 a leader of the Workers Confederation of Mexico (CTM)--a known protection union--claimed that he was negotiating a collective bargaining agreement to cover workers at a tire factory in San Luis Potosi that was not set to begin production until 2017. As of July, of 31 automotive industry plants, 27 had protection contracts with the CTM.

Independent unions, a few multinational corporations, and some labor lawyers and academics called on the government to institute legal reforms that would prohibit registration of collective bargaining agreements where the union cannot demonstrate support by a majority of workers or where workers had not ratified the content of the agreements. Many observers noted working conditions of a majority of workers were under the control of these contracts and the unrepresentative unions that negotiated them, and that the protection unions and contracts often prevented workers from fully exercising their labor rights as defined by law. These same groups advocated for workers to receive hard copies of existing collective bargaining agreements when they are hired.

According to several NGOs and unions, many workers faced procedural obstacles and various forms of intimidation (including physical violence) from protection union leaders, or employers supporting a protection union, in the lead-up to, during, and after bargaining-rights elections from other workers, union leaders, violent individuals hired by a company, or employers favoring a particular union. Some employers attempted to influence bargaining-rights elections through the illegal hiring of pseudo employees immediately prior to the election to vote for the company-controlled union.

Other intimidating and manipulative practices continued to be common, including dismissal of workers for labor activism. In November 2015 hundreds of employees at a transnational factory in Ciudad Juarez, Chihuahua, began protesting low wages, the arbitrary firings of 120 workers, and unacceptable working conditions. Civil society groups reported that management failed to provide either the promised day wage increase or the legally required Christmas bonus at the end of 2015. When workers attempted to organize to rectify these conditions, employers met them with mass firings, threats, and intimidation. Other complaints included sexual harassment and unsafe working conditions that exposed factory workers to hazardous chemicals without appropriate protective gear.

On August 22, one of the largest teacher unions (CNTE) began the school year by launching teacher strikes and setting up roadblocks to protest proposed education reforms. The government and CNTE engaged in numerous rounds of negotiations regarding the dispute following deadly clashes in June between teacher union-led protesters and federal police forces in Oaxaca that left eight civilians dead. CNTE members staged strikes in Oaxaca and Chiapas states, where 53 percent and 58 percent, respectively, of campuses did not open for the first day of school. CNTE was less successful in Guerrero and Michoacan states, where nearly all schools held classes. The CNTE blocked major roads and railways in Oaxaca and Chiapas to protest federal education reforms. On August 25, the Ministry of Education announced it would fire 1,255 teachers and school employees in Oaxaca and Guerrero who participated in the strikes and missed days of classes. As of September 6, authorities were processing 1,905 teachers for dismissal, including 1,600 from Oaxaca and the remainder from Chiapas and Michoacan.

Independent labor activists reported the requirement that the CABs approve strikes in advance gave the boards the power to show favoritism by determining which companies to protect from strikes. Few formal strikes occurred, but protests and informal work freezes were common. For instance, workers in "maquilas" (factories run by foreign-owned companies that manufacture goods for export) in Ciudad Juarez protested in January to gain support for the creation of an independent union.

b. Prohibition of Forced or Compulsory Labor

The law prohibits all forms of forced or compulsory labor, but the government did not effectively enforce the law. Penalties for conviction of forced labor violations range from five to 30 years' imprisonment and observers generally considered them sufficient to deter violations.

Forced labor persisted in the agricultural and industrial sectors, as well as in the informal sector. Women and children were subject to domestic servitude. Women, children, indigenous persons, and migrants (including men, women, and children) were the most vulnerable to forced labor. In November, 81 workers were freed by authorities from a situation of forced labor on a commercial farm in Coahuila.

In October 2015 municipal police rescued 49 persons held captive and forced to work 16 hours a day at a drug rehabilitation facility in Iztapalapa, Mexico City. The victims, mostly from indigenous groups, lived in overcrowded, unhealthy conditions and faced mistreatment and sexual exploitation. Some of the rescued laborers sent to hospitals suffered from malnutrition, dehydration, skin cuts, infections, and fractures.

Also see the Department of State's *Trafficking in Persons Report* at www.state.gov/j/tip/rls/tiprpt/.

c. Prohibition of Child Labor and Minimum Age for Employment

The constitution prohibits children under age 15 from working and allows those between ages 15 and 17 to work no more than six daytime hours in nonhazardous conditions daily, and only with parental permission. The law requires that children under age 18 must have a medical certificate in order to work. The minimum age for hazardous work is 18. The law prohibits minors from working in a broad list of hazardous and unhealthy occupations.

The government was reasonably effective in enforcing child labor laws in large and medium-sized companies, especially the maquila sector, and other industries under federal jurisdiction. Enforcement was inadequate in many small companies and in the agriculture and construction sectors and nearly absent in the informal sector, in which most child laborers worked.

With regard to inspections at the federal level, the SEDESOL, the PGR, and the National System for Integral Family Development have responsibility for enforcement of some aspects of child labor laws or intervention in cases where employers violated such laws. The STPS is responsible for carrying out child-labor inspections. Penalties for violations range from 16,780 pesos ($1,000) to 335,850 pesos ($20,000) but were not sufficiently enforced to deter violations.

In August authorities rescued six child laborers in Coahuila in the rural community of San Eugenio. Many of the victims in these cases came from the states of Veracruz and San Luis Potosi and reportedly worked at least nine hours daily, received insufficient food, and were forced to live in unhygienic conditions. In December 2015 authorities granted Oscar Lozano Chavez, the owner of the company involved in the case, house arrest due to health problems; he was monitored by an electronic bracelet. The court denied similar requests by three other defendants.

According to the 2013 INEGI survey, the most recent data available on child labor, the number of employed children between ages five and 17 remained at 2.5 million, or approximately 8.6 percent of the 29.3 million children in the country.

Of these children, 746,000 were between ages five and 13, and 1.8 million were between ages 14 and 17. Of employed children 30 percent worked in the agricultural sector in the harvest of melons, onions, cucumbers, eggplants, chili peppers, green beans, sugarcane, tobacco, coffee, and tomatoes. Other sectors with significant child labor included services (25 percent), retail sales (26 percent), manufacturing (13 percent), and construction (4 percent). On August 25, the government announced the percentage of children engaged in labor decreased from 11.5 percent of total children in 2007 to 7.5 percent in 2015.

d. Discrimination with Respect to Employment and Occupation

The law prohibits discrimination with respect to employment or occupation regarding "race, nationality age, religion, sex, political opinion, social status, handicap (or challenged capacity), economic status, health, pregnancy, language, sexual preference, or marital status." The law provides for labor protection for pregnant women.

The government did not effectively enforce these laws and regulations. Penalties for violations of the law included administrative remedies, such as reinstatement, payment of back wages, and fines (often calculated based on the employee's wages), and were not generally considered sufficient to deter violations. Discrimination in employment or occupation occurred against women, indigenous groups, persons with disabilities, LGBTI individuals, and migrant workers.

e. Acceptable Conditions of Work

The single general minimum wage was 73 pesos ($4.35) a day. Most formal sector workers received between one and three times the minimum wage. The National Council for the Evaluation of Social Development Policy estimated the poverty line at 90 pesos ($5.40) per day. The tripartite National Minimum Wage Commission, whose labor representatives largely represented protection unions and their interests, is responsible for establishing minimum salaries and continued to block increases that kept pace with inflation.

The law sets six eight-hour days and 48 hours per week as the legal workweek. Any work more than eight hours in a day is considered overtime, for which a worker receives double the hourly wage. After accumulating nine hours of overtime in a week, a worker earns triple the hourly wage. The law prohibits compulsory overtime. The law provides for eight paid public holidays and one week of paid annual leave after completing one year of work. The law requires employers to observe occupational safety and health regulations, issued jointly by the STPS and the Institute for Social Security. Legally mandated joint management and labor committees set standards and are responsible for overseeing workplace standards in plants and offices. Individual employees or unions may complain directly to inspectors or safety and health officials. By law workers may remove themselves from situations that endanger health or safety without jeopardy to their employment.

The STPS is responsible for enforcing labor laws and conducting inspections at workplaces. As of November 2015, there were 946 inspectors nationwide. This was sufficient to enforce compliance, and the STPS carried out inspections of workplaces throughout the year, using a questionnaire and other actions to identify victims of labor exploitation. Penalties for violations of wage, hours of work, or occupational safety and health laws range from 17,330 pesos ($1,030) to 335,940 pesos ($20,020) but were generally not sufficient to deter violations. Through its DECLARALAB self-evaluation tool, STPS had provided technical assistance to almost 4,000 registered workplaces to help them meet occupational safety and health regulations.

According to labor rights NGOs, employers in all sectors sometimes used the illegal "hours bank" approach--requiring long hours when the workload is heavy and cutting hours when it is light--to avoid compensating workers for overtime. This continued to be a common practice in the maquila sector, in which employers forced workers to take leave at low moments in the production cycle and oblige them to work, for example, during the Christmas holiday period, with no corresponding triple pay as mandated by law when workers opted for voluntary overtime on national holidays. Additionally, many companies evaded taxes and social security payments by employing workers informally, or by submitting falsified payroll records to the Mexican Social Security Institute. In 2013, the latest year for which such data are available, INEGI estimated 59 percent of the workforce was engaged in the informal economy.

Private recruitment agencies and individual recruiters violated the rights of temporary migrant workers recruited in the country to work abroad, primarily in the United States. Although the law requires these agencies to be registered, they often were unregistered. The STPS registry was out of date and limited in scope. Although a few large recruitments firms were registered, the registry included many defunct and nonexistent mid-sized firms, and few if any of the many small, independent recruiters. Although the government did not actively monitor or control the recruitment process, it reportedly was responsive in addressing complaints. There were also reports that registered agencies defrauded workers with impunity. Some temporary migrant workers were regularly charged illegal recruitment fees. According to a 2013 study conducted by the Migrant Worker Rights Center, 58 percent of 220 applicants interviewed had paid recruitment fees; half did not receive a copy of their job contract and took out loans to cover recruitment costs; and 10 percent paid recruitment fees for nonexistent jobs. The recruitment agents placed those who demanded their rights on blacklists and barred them from future employment opportunities. In 2015 the NGO Proyecto de Derechos Economicos, Sociales, y Culturales, or ProDESC, filed a collective criminal complaint with the government for recruitment fraud to demand an inspection of a recruitment agency. The government inspection resulted in a fine of 57,750 pesos ($3,500) levied against the recruiter.

News reports indicated that there were poor working conditions in some maquiladoras. These included low wages, contentious labor management, long work hours, unjustified dismissals, the lack of social security benefits, unsafe workplaces, and the lack of freedom of association. Many women working in the industry reported suffering some form of abuse. Most maquilas hired employees through outsourcing with few social benefits.